There Must Be a Better Way

Walking in Salvation

Book One

Walking with Jesus

Becoming the Best Me I Can Be

Pamela D White

A publication of Blooming Desert Ministries

ISBN 978-1-7370802-0-6 (sc print)
ISBN 978-1-7370802-1-3 (ebook)

IngramSparks Publishing (Ingram: Lightning Source, LLC)

One Ingram Blvd., La Vergne, TN 37086

Publishing Note: Publishing style capitalizes certain pronouns in Scriptures that refer to the Father, Son, and Holy Spirit, and may differ from other publishing styles. **All emphasis in the Scriptures' quotations is the authors.** The name satan and related names are not capitalized as the author's preference not to acknowledge him, even though it violates grammatical rules.

PDW PUBLICATIONS

Dedication

This book series is dedicated to you.

Everyone has opportunities to become a better version of themselves. My prayer is that this book series helps you on that journey. The Lord loves you so much He desires an intimate relationship with you. You are special to Him and He loves spending time with you. Walking and talking with Jesus every day should be the norm, not the exception. Life can bring difficult circumstances and situations. When you walk with Jesus, life events, are not only manageable but can be turned for your good.

"And we know that all things work together for good to those who love God, to those who are the called according to His purpose," Romans 8:28.

Come with me into this exploration of how you can develop a relationship with Jesus and walk with Him every day. This is an opportunity to become a better you.

Acknowledgments

The Great Commission given by our Lord and Savior Jesus Christ noted in Matthew 28:16-20 is my inspiration for this publication. Verses 19-20 state, *"Go therefore and make disciples of all the nations, baptizing them in the name of the Father and of the Son and of the Holy Spirit, teaching them to observe all things that I have commanded you; and lo, I am with you always, even to the end of the age."* This verse is the very basis for missionary work all over the globe. I have been blessed to be able to serve in a few of those missions. Missions are an amazing experience. I came to realize though that everyone cannot always do all the parts commanded in these verses. I can't always go. I didn't often get to baptize. What I realized was that I can do my part in teaching to observes the truths of the Scriptures. My desire to fulfill the teaching part of the Great Commission was the inspiration for this work. My pastor, Bishop Larry Taylor, and First Lady Desetra Taylor allowed our church to use these Bible studies in our New Life Discipleship classes for nearly twenty years. The work has also been used in prison ministries in central Illinois for as many years. The teaching has proven effective in changing many lives and discipling the children of God. Thank you, Bishop and First Lady, for teaching a balanced spiritual and natural life so I could complete this project and see the impact of the work on people's lives.

Bishop positioned me to be the director of New Life Ministries Discipleship for several years. New Life classes were designed to teach those new to Christianity or new to the church the foundational truths needed to build a solid life in Christ. During that time, this work was fine-tuned with the help and input from the dedicated, gifted, and anointed New Life teachers Minister Retta Smith, Minister James Smith, Minister Debby Henkel, Dr. Terry Husband, Minister Char-Michelle McDowell, Minister Yvonne Smith, Minister Herbert Smyer, and Professor Susan Gibson along with the encouragement and guidance of Dr. Chequita Brown and community service advocate Minister Patricia Turner. I also want to give a shout-out to Dr. Wanda Turner, nationally acclaimed minister, teacher, prophet, life coach, mentor, and best-selling author, who continued to encourage me to just publish the thing! Thanks to all of you. Each of you has made a significant impact on my life.

My dear friend and mentor, First Lady Marshell Wickware, supported the project and pushed me to publish it for years. Thanks for not giving up on me!

My life-long friend, Robin McClallen, thank you for all your support, input, and encouraging me to publish something. You have been instrumental in making me an author.

A special thanks to my husband, Brian K. White, for his patience and prayers as I spent hours and hours researching, writing, and rewriting. Thanks, BW for your love and support!

Most of all thank you to the Holy Spirit and my Lord and Savior Jesus Christ. I present this work in obedience and honor to You.

Contents

Book One

There Must Be a Better Way
Walking in Salvation

OBJECTIVE

This lesson provides a Biblical basis for the foundation of salvation. It is intended to assist you in understanding God's plan for you, which is first to reconcile you to Himself. Through Jesus Christ, His people progressively grow in liberty from a selfish nature into harmony with God. People are born selfish. That's what sin-nature is. You've seen those shows about Extreme MakeOver or Extreme Couponing. Sin-nature is about being Extreme Selfish. You just can't help it, but He will help you become more and more unselfish so you can better serve Him and others. This lesson will equip you with the tools to walk out your salvation.

MEMORY VERSES

"For whoever calls on the name of the Lord shall be saved." Romans 10:13

"For all have sinned and fall short of the glory of God." Romans 3:23

There Must Be a Better Way
Introduction

By definition, the word "salvation" means **DELIVERANCE FROM THE POWER OF SIN**; redemption or having eternal life. The Bible is full of references to salvation. Old Testament salvation is often referred to as deliverance. Many would seek salvation when faced with danger, oppression from the enemy, or the healing of sickness and disease. The salvation we are discussing today includes the same characterizations as the Old Testament with the added spiritual benefit of freedom from sin.

What is Salvation?

God's perfect plan for you never included sin or death. When God created the earth, He created man (anytime you see 'man' in this book, it is referring to all humankind, including men and women) and set him in the perfect paradise called the Garden of Eden. Deception entered the garden in the form of a serpent. Adam listened to the lies and believed the deception. His choice was in direct disobedience to the instruction of God. Disobedience always separates God and man. Adam sold his soul to the devil at that moment. From that point forward, the old serpent owned man. Here are the scriptures of man's creation and fall. I encourage you to read Genesis chapters 1-3 for the entire account.

"And God said, Let us make man in our image, after our likeness: and let them have dominion over the fish of the sea, and over the fowl of the air, and over the cattle, and over all the earth, and over every creeping thing that creepeth upon the earth. So God created man in his own image, in the image of God created he him; male and female created he them. And God blessed them, and God said unto them, Be fruitful, and multiply, and replenish the earth, and subdue it: and have dominion over the fish of the sea, and over the fowl of the air, and over every living thing that moveth upon the earth. And God said, Behold, I have given you every herb bearing seed, which is upon the

face of all the earth, and every tree, in the which is the fruit of a tree yielding seed; to you it shall be for meat. And to every beast of the earth, and to every fowl of the air, and to every thing that creepeth upon the earth, wherein there is life, I have given every green herb for meat: and it was so. And God saw every thing that he had made, and behold, it was very good. And the evening and the morning were the sixth day," Genesis 1:26-31 KJV.

"And the Lord God took the man, and put him into the garden of Eden to dress it and to keep it," Genesis 2:15 KJV.

"Now the serpent was more subtle than any beast of the field which the Lord God had made. And he said unto the woman, Yea, hath God said, Ye shall not eat of every tree of the garden? And the woman said unto the serpent, We may eat of the fruit of the trees of the garden: But of the fruit of the tree which is in the midst of the garden, God hath said, Ye shall not eat of it, neither shall ye touch it, lest ye die. And the serpent said unto the woman, Ye shall not surely die: For God doth know that in the day ye eat thereof, then your eyes shall be opened, and ye shall be as gods, knowing good and evil. And when the woman saw that the tree was good for food, and that it was pleasant to the eyes, and a tree to be desired to make one wise, she took of the fruit thereof, and did eat, and gave also unto her husband with her; and he did eat. And the eyes of them both were opened, and they knew that they were naked; and they sewed fig leaves together, and made themselves aprons," Genesis 3:1-7 KJV.

Every child since that moment has been born into sin, including you. The good news is that Jesus came to redeem or buy you back out of sin and offer you the fullness of inheritance as part of God's family. The price paid for you was the blood of God's Son. That's a pretty hefty cost. We will talk about this more throughout this lesson.

SUMMARY OF SALVATION

- Salvation is a plan developed by God to provide people deliverance from sin and spiritual death. You already know about the body dying. Most have experienced the death of someone you know and/or love. Spiritual death is a little different. To be spiritually dead is to have your spirit eternally separated from God. This is way worse than physical death.

- The salvation plan offers the gift of repentance. Repentance is the opportunity to transform your mind, which results in a total change of actions. It is turning absolutely away from sin.

- God provides a picture of deliverance and salvation when Israel gained freedom from Egypt in the book of Exodus. The Israelites were slaves in a foreign land, Egypt. They sought freedom from their taskmaster. God sent Moses to lead them in their deliverance into freedom. (You can find the account of their deliverance from Egypt in the book of Exodus in chapters 1-12). Their story is a depiction of what Jesus does for you. Sin is your taskmaster. Sin binds you in slavery. Jesus bought your deliverance into freedom from sin.

- Jesus Christ is the source of salvation. It is His perfect sacrifice that paid the ransom for your freedom and bridges the gap to restore a relationship with the Father.

How Do I Know I'm Saved?

There was a preacher that once said, "You can sit in a garage and call yourself a car. That doesn't make you a car." Likewise, you can live your entire life calling yourself Christian and never receive deliverance from a life of sin. You can be a 'good' person, do great things, help others, go to church, call yourself a Christian and yet never be Christian. Here are some markers that will help you know if you are saved, born again, renewed, and redeemed.

- You have confessed Jesus as your Lord and Savior.

   "That if you confess with your mouth the Lord Jesus, and believe in your heart that God has raised Him from the dead, you will be saved. For with the heart one believes unto righteousness, and with the mouth confession is made unto salvation," Romans 10:9-10.

- You believe Jesus Christ died on the cross, was buried, and raised from the dead. In many liturgical churches, there is a recitation that occurs called the Apostles Creed. You may be familiar with it if you spent any time in a denominational church. It is an excellent declaration of the confession one believes when receiving salvation. It goes like this:

I believe in God the Father Almighty, Maker of heaven and earth. And in Jesus Christ, His only Son, our Lord; Who was conceived by the Holy Spirit; Born of the Virgin Mary; Suffered under Pontius Pilate; Was crucified, dead and buried; He descended into Hell; The third day He rose again from the dead; He ascended into heaven; And sits on the right hand of God the Father Almighty; From thence He shall come to judge the living and the dead. I believe in the Holy Spirit; The Holy Christian Church, the Communion of Saints; The Forgiveness of sins; The Resurrection of the body; And the life everlasting. Amen.

Great declaration, right? Thousands declare it every Sunday morning. The trouble is many don't believe it or live it. Salvation makes it possible to not only speak it but live like you believe it.

• Additional scriptures for your personal study time. I encourage you to look them up yourself and make a note of what they reveal to you.

"Whoever confesses that Jesus is the Son of God, God abides in him, and he in God," 1 John 4:15.

"Jesus answered and said to him, "Most assuredly, I say to you, unless one is born again, he cannot see the kingdom of God." Nicodemus said to Him, "How can a man be born when he is old? Can he enter a second time into his mother's womb and be born?" Jesus answered, "Most assuredly, I say to you, unless one is born of water and the Spirit, he cannot enter the kingdom of God. That which is born of the flesh is flesh, and that which is born of the Spirit is spirit. Do not marvel that I said to you, 'You must be born again,'" John 3:3-7.

"Therefore He is also able to save to the uttermost those who come to God through Him, since He always lives to make intercession for them," Hebrews 7:25.

What Changes When I Receive Christ's Salvation?

Many changes begin when you choose to believe. Two of the most prominent confirming changes are these:

- You become a **NEW** creation in Christ. No longer are you subject and a slave to sin. No longer do you have to live broken and hurting. You can live free and whole. Your body still looks the same. Initially, your mind might have many of the same thoughts. However, your spirit is brand new, reborn, recreated. Those old thoughts you have sometimes just don't fit anymore.

    "Therefore if any one is in Christ, he is a new creature: old things have passed away; behold, all things have become new," 2 Corinthians 5:17.

- The Spirit of God bears witness with your spirit that you are now a child of God. You may or may not have had a good natural father. As a child of God, you now have the perfect Father and He will never leave you. 'Bearing witness' means that God declares you are now His. You belong to Him and He no one else. It's like a momma bear defending her cubs. He calls you His even when you struggle with believing or mess up. You are His and if you act like you don't remember that, He will not let you forget.

"The Spirit Himself bears witness with our spirit that we are children of God," Romans 8:16.

Why Do I Need Salvation?

The foundation of your Christian belief rests on the teaching of salvation. As was noted at the beginning of this lesson, the need for salvation goes back to the fall of man in the Garden of Eden (Genesis 3). Adam and Eve's disobedience led all of humankind into a permanent state of sin and corruption. The consequences of their actions were both spiritual and physical death, breaking fellowship with God. This state of sin and death applies to every person, including you and me.

SEPARATION FROM GOD

Broken fellowship means you lose access to the Father. Your communication pipeline breaks. It isn't just damaged or leaking. It becomes completely broken. There is no flow.

- Sinfulness separates you from God. God's plan is to spend time with humankind daily as He did with Adam and Eve in the garden. When Adam disobeyed by eating the forbidden fruit, he set the destiny of all humankind to be born into sin. You don't have a choice. It is the law of life. Consider the law of gravity. You can't turn gravity off. It just is, and it is always working. You can temporarily defy gravity. Airplanes do this all the time. You can't turn sin-nature off. It just is. You can temporarily look like you are defying sin just like an airplane looks like it is temporarily defying gravity. If the engines turn off, the plane comes down. You can pretend you don't have sin, but the second you let your guard down, sin will rule. Airplanes can't break the atmospheric barrier, but the Space Shuttle can. When the space shuttle breaks the atmospheric barrier, it is free from gravity. You can't break the sin barrier, but Jesus can. When Jesus broke the sin barrier, He gave you a choice. You have the choice to stay living with sin-nature or to become free from that bondage and separation from God and soar high and free.

"For all have sinned and fall short of the glory of God," Romans 3:23.

"For the wages of sin is death, but the gift of God is eternal life in Christ Jesus our Lord," Romans 6:23.

- The sinning soul has a fateful, predetermined state. Scripture makes it clear. If you stay in a sinful state, you will not just die once. You will die twice and the second death will be painful and final. The first death is when your body dies. The second death is when your soul and spirit experience permanent separation from God. This is a far worse punishment than having your body die. The eternity you live is up to you—eternity with the Lord or an eternity forever separated from God.

"But the cowardly, the unbelieving, the vile, the murderers, and sexually immoral, those who practice magic arts, the idolaters, and all liars, they will be consigned to the lake of burning sulfur. This is the second death," Revelation 21:8 NIV.

How Do I Correct a Sinful Life?

As hard as you might try, you cannot correct any sin. You can make an attempt, but it will be fruitless no matter how much good you do. The only way to correct sin is by receiving Christ into your life. Then **for** Him rather than **for** yourself. Jesus is the bridge to the Father. It is His righteousness that takes you from a life of sinful choices to a life of righteous choices. You can be righteous, but only through the sacrifice of Christ. The cross of Christ bridges the gap between our Holy God and sinful man.

Walking in Righteousness

Being born-again, saved, or accepting salvation puts you in a position to walk in righteousness.

- Righteousness is being in right standing with God. What does right standing mean? It means you accepted Jesus' salvation and adoption into God's family. You have become a new creation in Him and are becoming who God created you to be. You believe Jesus shed His blood for you.

  "For He made Him who knew no sin to be sin for us, that we might become the righteousness of God in Him," 2 Corinthians 5:21.

- Righteousness is believing, trusting, and obeying God with child-like faith.

  "Assuredly, I say to you, unless you are converted and become as little children, you will by no means enter the kingdom of heaven. Therefore, whoever humbles himself as this little child is the greatest in the kingdom of heaven," Matthew 18:3-4.

- Righteousness is walking in justice and salvation. You will do good works not to earn righteousness, which is impossible, but you do good works because you are righteous in Christ.

"Therefore, O king, let my advice be acceptable to you; break off your sins by being righteous, and your iniquities by showing mercy to the poor. Perhaps there may be a lengthening of your prosperity," Daniel 4:27.

NO LONGER A SLAVE BUT A SERVANT

Sin put you in slavery. You had no choice but to be subject to sin. Sin trapped you. Christ conquered sin and death. You **NO LONGER HAVE TO BE A SLAVE TO SIN OR DEATH, BUT CAN LIVE FREE** as a willing servant of God and righteousness.

"Knowing this, that our old man was crucified with Him, that the body of sin might be done away with, that we should no longer be slaves of sin. For he who has died has been freed from sin. Now if we died with Christ, we believe that we shall also live with Him, knowing that Christ, having been raised from the dead, dies no more. Death no longer has dominion over Him. For the death that He died, He died to sin once for all; but the life that He lives, He lives to God. Likewise you also, reckon yourselves to be dead indeed to sin, but alive to God in Christ Jesus our Lord. Therefore do not let sin reign in your mortal body, that you should obey it in its lusts. And do not present your members as instruments of unrighteousness to sin, but present yourselves to God as being alive from the dead, and your members as instruments of righteousness to God. For sin shall not have dominion over you, for you are not under law but under grace," Romans 6:6-14.

- To no longer be a slave to sin, you must confess your sins to God. He already knows what your sins are, but He wants you to know what they are and to expose the sin by confession so it loses its

26

power. Part of the power of sin is in hiding it. Once you confess to God, its power loosens its grip on you.

- Repent: repentance is to do a 180o turn from whatever sin is attempting to rule in your life. Stop. Turn, change your thinking, and don't look back. You can use that mess from your past to push you into your future like a swimmer does when they push off the side of a pool. Allow it to propel you into your destiny.

- You have a choice. You can continue to sin, or you can choose to transform your life. It's really up to you.

Transformation

You have renewed relationship and fellowship with the Lord when you accept the salvation offered by Jesus Christ. You become a new creation in Christ. Because of salvation, you set your life to begin a **LIFE-LONG TRANSFORMATION**. The result is that you become more like Christ in the following ways:

- You represent Christ to others. When others see you fulfilling your destiny in Christ, your relationship with Jesus draws them into a relationship with Him as well.

  "Now then we are ambassadors for Christ, as though God did beseech you by us: we pray you in Christ's stead, be ye reconciled to God. For he hath made him to be sin for us, who knew no sin; that we might be made the righteousness of God in him," 2 Corinthians 5:20-21 KJV.

- You can show unconditional love. In your humanity, it is impossible to show unconditional love. With Christ in your life, you can express unconditional love toward others.

  "For God so loved the world, that he gave his only begotten Son, that whoever believes in him should not perish, but have everlasting life," John 3:16.

- You can live born again—renewed—having a fresh start on life. You will still remember your old life, but you live out your destiny/your future in the fullness that God intended from the moment He began to weave you together.

"Being born again, not of corruptible seed, but of incorruptible, by the word of God, which liveth and abideth for ever," 1 Peter 1:23 KJV.

- You can confess that there is no other name but Jesus that can save you.

"Neither is there salvation in any other: for there is none other name under heaven given among men, whereby we must be saved," Acts 4:12 KJV.

- You no longer have to live with the condemnation of sin. Sin has a habit of putting a heavy yoke of condemnation on you. Condemnation is blame, criticism, strong disapproval, and even punishment. It is a heavy burden and often comes with a feeling of guilt. Condemnation never comes from the Lord. You may, however, experience conviction from the Lord. Conviction shows you the sin but doesn't condemn you for the sin. The gift of repentance comes with conviction, so you transform. Simply put, condemnation brings death; conviction brings life.

"There is therefore now no condemnation to them which are in Christ Jesus, who walk not after the flesh, but after the Spirit," Romans 8:1 KJV.

Understanding Salvation

God created man as a three-part being, and salvation affects every part. You may have heard the description that you are a spirit that has a soul and lives in a body. **Your body** is the physical you. It experiences pain, pleasure, and other sensations experienced through your five senses. **Your soul** comprises your mind, will, and emotions. Prior to salvation, your thoughts are generated from your soul. You experienced all your 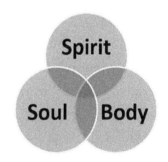 emotions through your soul. You made decisions through your soul experiences guided by your emotions. **Your spirit** is the piece of you that connects to God. It is the part of God that He breathed into you when He created you. Until you connect to God through salvation, it lies mostly dormant while longing to reconnect with the Creator. Salvation is not a one-time event, but a complete lifestyle makeover. Receiving salvation begins a process that includes the restoration of the soul, the regeneration of the spirit, and the transfiguration of the body. Living in salvation alters your day-to-day choices and brings your life into balance. Though this lesson looks at spirit, soul, and body separately, it is important to know that although each part has a different function; they work together and can affect the other parts dramatically. For instance, a wounded soul may manifest those wounds as diseases or illnesses in your body. You are a three-part being with the three parts intricately entwined. It's important to make sure all three parts are healthy and whole to live a balanced, healthy life. Let's take a more in-depth look at how salvation affects your three parts.

SALVATION OF THE SPIRIT IS JUSTIFICATION

Justification is the act of being made righteous in the sight of God. Prior to salvation, when God looked upon you, your sin was evident. The justification that occurs in salvation is the change from sin-nature to divine possibilities. When a person receives Christ as their personal Savior, the blood Christ shed on the cross becomes a covering washing away sin. From that moment, when God looks down on you, He sees the blood of Christ covering you — not your sins. It is being 'justified' — just-as-if-I'd never sinned — this is the amazing, beautiful truth of salvation. Christ takes all your sin and removes it as far as the east is from the west.

"He has removed our sins as far from us as the east is from the west," Psalm 103:12 NLT.

Sin is visible no more in your life. This doesn't mean you never sin again, but now you have the power of the blood to repent and remove any sin committed. Be careful, though. That does not mean you can sin freely and ask for forgiveness later. The scriptures are clear on that point.

"For sin shall not have dominion over you: for ye are not under the law, but under grace. What then? Shall we sin, because we are not under the law, but under grace? God forbid. Know ye not, that to whom ye yield yourselves servants to obey, his servants ye are to whom ye obey; whether of sin unto death, or of obedience unto righteousness? But God be thanked, that ye were the servants of sin, but ye have obeyed from the heart that form of doctrine which was delivered you. Being then made free from sin, ye became the servants of righteousness," Romans 6:14-18 KJV.

Justification is **INSTANT**. Eternal life is the result. The Judge of all things bangs His gavel and declares over your life — NOT GUILTY. Christ took your punishment and paid for your sin to allow you freedom.

"Therefore by the deeds of the law there shall no flesh be justified in his sight: for by the law is the knowledge of sin. But now the righteousness of God without the law is manifested, being witnessed by the law and the prophets; Even the righteousness of God which is by faith of Jesus Christ unto all and upon all them that believe: for there is no difference: For all have sinned, and come short of the glory of God; Being justified freely by his grace through the redemption that is in Christ Jesus: Whom God hath set forth to be a propitiation through faith in his blood, to declare his righteousness for the remission of sins that are past, through the forbearance of God; To declare, I say, at this time his righteousness: that he might be just, and the justifier of him which believeth in Jesus," Romans 3:20-26 KJV.

- Justification changes your nature from human to divine—you are born again. *"I will give you a new heart and put a new spirit within you,"* Ezekiel 36:26 NLT.

- Justification is a gift of the cross. You cannot earn justification.

"For if by one man's offence death reigned by one; much more they which receive abundance of grace and of the gift of righteousness shall reign in life by one, Jesus Christ. Therefore as by the offence of one judgment came upon all men to condemnation; even so by the righteousness of one the free gift came upon all men unto justification of life," Romans 5:17-18 KJV.

SALVATION OF THE SOUL IS SANCTIFICATION

Sanctification is the **PROCESS** of being made holy. It is being set apart for holy and righteous works.

- Sanctification is the separation from the seduction of sin. Seduction of sin comes through temptation and ungodly desires. It's enticing and deceitful. Sanctification separates you from those seductions.

   "Mortify therefore your members which are upon the earth; fornication, uncleanness, inordinate affection, evil concupiscence, and covetousness, which is idolatry: For which things' sake the wrath of God cometh on the children of disobedience: In the which ye also walked some time, when ye lived in them. But now ye also put off all these; anger, wrath, malice, blasphemy, filthy communication out of your mouth. Lie not one to another, seeing that ye have put off the old man with his deeds; And have put on the new man, which is renewed in knowledge after the image of him that created him," Colossians 3:5-10 KJV.

- Sanctification is progressive. It takes time and commitment.

   "I am crucified with Christ: nevertheless I live; yet not I, but Christ liveth in me: and the life which I now live in the flesh I live by the

faith of the Son of God, who loved me, and gave himself for me," Galatians 2:20 KJV.

- Sanctification describes a justified person actively involved in submitting to God's will, resisting sin, seeking holiness, and becoming balanced and godly.

  "How much more shall the blood of Christ, who through the eternal Spirit offered himself without spot to God, purge your conscience from dead works to serve the living God?" Hebrews 9:14 KJV.

- Philippians 2:12 describes sanctification when it states you must *"Work out your salvation with fear and trembling,"* NASB.

- Sanctification is about building Christian character day by day as you allow the work of the Holy Spirit in your life.

  "Therefore lay aside all filthiness and overflow of wickedness, and receive with meekness the implanted word, which is able to save your souls," James 1:21.

All of this sounds like work, right? It's really about choices. Every day, you will have choices to make regarding living a sanctified life. Do I lie or tell the truth, enter the gossip, get angry, tell a filthy joke, or speak life instead? You will have choices every day of your life. Initially, some choices may seem difficult, but the more you choose the 'What would Jesus do' choice, the easier the next choice is to make.

"This day I call the heavens and the earth as witnesses against you that I have set before you life and death, blessings and curses. Now choose life, so that you and your children may live 20 and that you may love the Lord your God, listen to his voice, and hold fast to him. For the Lord is your life," Deuteronomy 30:19-20.

SALVATION OF THE BODY IS GLORIFICATION

Glorification is God's final removal of sin from His children. It is when you, a child of God, realize the glory of God. It is when you can worship and praise God with all purity. His majesty, holiness, praise, and honor are manifest in His people and they are completely unhindered to access the presence of God. You will be unhindered because sin no longer exists.

- Glorification means sin no longer exists on any level in your eternal condition. You change from mortal to immortal. How cool is that?

- Glorification is a future and final work of God. It's something to look forward to as a person who loves the Lord and has become a child of the living God. When you are born again, you begin your transformation to be more like Jesus and begin living for eternity with Him. Glorification is the final step that completes your transformation. This occurs at the last trumpet during the end times (See Apocalypse Now).

- Glorification is the physical dominion over the effects of sin. You will have a body that no longer tries to rule over your life. No more sickness, no more pain, no more tempting desires, no sin-nature within the physical body. Glorification transforms your mortal, physical body into an **ETERNAL** physical body in which you will dwell forever. Yes, it's trade-in time! You get a whole new model to dwell in, You 2.0, and sin is no longer a battle.

  "It is sown a natural body, it is raised a spiritual body. There is a natural body, there is a spiritual body," 1 Corinthians 15:44.

"But let me reveal to you a wonderful secret. We will not all die, but we will all be transformed! It will happen in a moment, in the blink of an eye, when the last trumpet is blown. For when the trumpet sounds, those who have died will be raised to live forever. And we who are living will also be transformed. For our dying bodies must be transformed into bodies that will never die; our mortal bodies must be transformed into immortal bodies," 1 Corinthians 15:51-53 NLT.

SALVATION TRANSFORMATION – SPIRIT, SOUL, AND BODY

Here is a quick breakdown of what we just discussed for quick reference.

	Spirit	Soul	Body
Tense of Salvation	Justification Initial	Sanctification Current	Glorification Final
When?	Instant	Progressive	Future
What?	Transform from human to divine nature	Building character on the foundation of divine nature	Transforms mortal body to eternal body
How?	Gift of the Cross	Requires personal choice	Reward of positive choices

The Finished Work of Christ

The finished work of Christ began when the cross ended. Jesus stated to all in John 19:30 *"It is finished."* Jesus' work on the cross was perfect and complete. He finished all that He came to do. The Mighty Warrior conquered sin and death. His sacrifice made a way for your reconciliation with Father God. He made a way for you to live in joy and hope instead of despair and pain. It truly is finished. Here are the works Christ completed through His process of sacrifice on the cross, His death, His burial, and His resurrection.

- **Jesus is the Atonement**

    Atonement is being reconciled or restoring a relationship with God. Jesus made reconciliation with Father God possible through His death and sacrificial blood. There is only one person who is qualified to atone for man's sin and reconcile man back to God. That person had to be sinless. His name is Jesus Christ. He became High Priest and offered up the ultimate, perfect, sinless sacrifice. Jesus' atonement makes it possible to develop a relationship with Father, Son, and Holy Spirit.

    "And not only so, but we also joy in God through our Lord Jesus Christ, by whom we have now received the atonement. Why, as by one man

sin entered into the world, and death by sin; and so death passed on all men, for that all have sinned," Romans 5:11-12 AKJV.

God desires a relationship with you, but sin breaks that relationship and separates you from God. Atonement pays the penalty of sin and buys you back from the entrapment of sin so you can be one with the Father.

"For it pleased the Father that in Him all the fullness should dwell, and by Him to reconcile all things to Himself, by Him, whether things on earth or things in heaven, having made peace through the blood of His cross," Colossians 1:19-20.

When Adam and Eve disobeyed God, they sold out to sin. They also sold all the rest of humankind to sin. There is only one thing that could buy back this priceless, precious commodity and that is **INNOCENT BLOOD**. That was the price. Legally, the payment required for your freedom was innocent blood. Jesus shed innocent blood on the cross at Calvary to buy you back. He loved you that much. It was so vitally important to Him to provide a way for you to fellowship with Father, Son, and Holy Spirit once again without the burden of sin or the bondage of the chains of darkness. His blood and death paid the price for your sin. Because of His sacrifice, you can be one with Christ and enter freely into a relationship with your Creator.

- **Redemption**. Jesus is your redemption. Redemption means 'to buy or purchase.' Jesus bought you from the hands of the enemy with the highest cost, His very life, and His sacrificial blood.

"For as much as you know that you were not redeemed with corruptible things as silver and gold, from your vain conversation received by

tradition from your fathers; but with the precious blood of Christ, as of a lamb without blemish and without spot," 1 Peter 1:18-19 AKJV.

- **Propitiation.** Sin makes God angry. He created you in love because He desired a relationship with you. Sin takes you away from Him and that makes God angry. He gave you so many blessings and offers you an incredible life. When sin is chosen over a relationship with Him, it isn't good. His anger must be satisfied. There must be an exchange or atonement. A price must be paid. Propitiation means 'to satisfy the anger of God.' Jesus' sacrifice on the cross is propitiation or the appeasement of God's anger.

"Being justified freely by His grace through the redemption that is in Christ Jesus, whom God set forth as a propitiation by His blood, through faith, to demonstrate His righteousness, because in His forbearance God had passed over the sins that were previously committed, to demonstrate at the present time His righteousness, that He might be just and the justifier of the one who has faith in Jesus," Romans 3:24-26.

"Who is a liar but he that denies that Jesus is the Christ? He is antichrist that denies the Father and the Son," 1 John 2:22.

- **Reconciliation** means 'to restore harmony and fellowship.' Remember that sin separates you from the Father. Fellowship with the Father became possible through Jesus. The Lord desires a relationship with you so much that He sent His Son to bring you back home to Him. You are that important to Almighty God.

"Therefore, if anyone is in Christ, he is a new creation; old things have passed away; behold, all things have become new. Now all things are

of God, who has reconciled us to Himself through Jesus Christ, and has given us the ministry of reconciliation, that is, that God was in Christ reconciling the world to Himself, not imputing their trespasses to them, and has committed to us the word of reconciliation. Now then, we are ambassadors for Christ, as though God were pleading through us: we implore you on Christ's behalf, be reconciled to God. For He made Him who knew no sin to be sin for us, that we might become the righteousness of God in Him," 2 Corinthians 5:17-21.

You Are an Eternal Being

Eternity is a tough concept for the human mind to conceive. Time limits the mind, which makes thinking in an eternal state challenging. Eternity is not an endless concession of years. Time doesn't even exist in eternity, so there are no years. It is a perpetual life. Eternal life is a gift to the believer. God granted Jesus the authority over all people that He might give eternal life to all those given to Him.

"As thou hast given him power over all flesh, that he should give eternal life to as many as thou hast given him. And this is life eternal, that they might know thee the only true God, and Jesus Christ, whom thou hast sent," John 17:2-3 KJV.

John 17 does not talk about how many years eternity is because time ceases to exist, but John does tell us what eternity is like. It's a life more concerned with quality than quantity. You are walking in eternal life when you know the only true God, Jesus Christ. Eternity is forever. It's endless and you can start living in eternity today.

Your life in Christ is eternal. Many in the world teach death is the final blow. Death is not the end, but the next step to a different life. Death is hard for those left behind because death was never supposed to be part of the life experience. God planned that humans would live forever with Him. That's why He put the Tree of Life in the Garden of Eden for man to eat. Sin destroyed that and destined humans to die in sin. Jesus broke the bondage of sin and death so you don't have to die in sin, but you can live to live again. You are already an eternal creation.

YOUR SPIRIT AND SOUL KEEP ON LIVING after death. Yes, your body dies, but it has to so you can get your new glorified body. You have the power to decide where you will live when you pass from this life to eternal life. These are some things to know about eternity so you can choose wisely.

CHARACTERISTICS OF LIVING ETERNALLY

Eternity is existing always. Your body dies, but your spirit and soul live on forever.

"And I give them eternal life; and they shall never perish; neither shall anyone snatch them out of My hand," John 10:28.

"For God so loved the world, that He gave His only begotten Son, that whoever believes in Him should not perish but have everlasting life," John 3:16.

Eternity is an opportunity to know God on a different, more intense level. No longer is God a mystery. You can see Him face to face. (Quality of relationship, not quantity of time.)

"And this is life eternal, that they might know thee the only true God, and Jesus Christ, whom thou hast sent," John 17:3 KJV.

Passing from this life offers two choices – Eternal Blessing or Eternal Punishment. Choose wisely grasshopper.

"He that believeth on the Son hath everlasting life: and he that believeth not the Son shall not see life; but the wrath of God abideth on him," John 3:36 KJV.

John 3 also lets you know you can start living eternity today. Eternity is not limited to time. You step into your eternity when you decide to believe in Jesus because eternity is not about your future years, but about your standing with God in Christ as noted in John 17:3 above.

Below are scriptures on eternity for you to read and study so you can better understand what eternity is and make a quality decision on how you want to live it. Read these scriptures and write what you learn about eternity.

Genesis 4

Job 33:8-9

Psalm 51; 103:3-12; 141:3-4

Titus 1:2

Hebrews 6:18; 10:17

Jeremiah 31:34-35

Proceed with caution!
The next part has the power
to change your life forever!

Confession of Faith

Once you make a confession of faith and receive Jesus as your personal Savior, He will forever become your friend, guide, lover, counselor, savior, mentor, king, deliverer, peace, compassion, and so much more.

PRAYER OF SALVATION

If you have not invited Jesus into your life and you want to, then here is a prayer for you to help guide you toward salvation. If you have already received salvation, then this prayer can be a guide for when you lead others to the Lord.

Lord, I come to you in the name of Jesus. I acknowledge to You I am a sinner. I am sorry for my sins and the life that I have lived. I need your forgiveness. I believe that your only begotten Son Jesus Christ shed His precious blood on the cross and died for my sins. I will turn from my sin. You said in Romans 10:9 that if I confess the Lord my God and believe in my hearts that God raised Jesus from the dead, I would be saved.

I confess Jesus as the Lord of my soul. With my heart, I believe God raised Jesus from the dead. I accept Jesus Christ as my personal Savior, and according to His Word, I am saved.

Thank you, Jesus, for your unlimited grace, which has saved me from my sins. I thank you Jesus that your grace never leads to license but always leads to repentance. Therefore, Lord Jesus, transform my life so that I may bring glory and honor to you alone and not to myself.

Thank you, Jesus, for dying for me and giving me eternal life. Amen.

Tools to Help You Walk Out Your Salvation

READ the Bible. This is an important part of walking with Christ. How can you know someone if you don't communicate with them? The Lord wrote you a love letter. It is full of dramatic family history, life lessons, guidance for daily living, explanations of why things happen, and expressions of tenderness and love. It's called the Holy Bible. If you aren't sure how to read and study the Bible, please see book seven, *Love Letters from God* in the *Walking with Jesus* series.

"Oh, how I love Your law! It is my meditation all the day," Psalm 119:97.

"May my meditation be sweet to Him; I will be glad in the Lord," Psalm 104:34.

PRAYER which is communicating with God. Prayer is not just throwing your needs and wants toward heaven, but having a conversation with Him. You talk, He listens. Then He talks and you listen. You find out how each one feels about different things. Then He goes and works on what you have asked and you go do what He asked. It's a dialog, a discussion, a tête-à-tête. You and Him - all alone working out things. You can and should do this all day long. Check in frequently, even if it's just saying thanks for something. If you need help with prayer, please see book eight, *Time in the Garden* in the *Walking with Jesus* series.

"Pray without ceasing," 1 Thessalonians 5:17 KJV.

FELLOWSHIP with other believers. That means to worship God with other people. It means to go to the church picnic or invite some fellow Christians over to your house to play some boardgame and eat some pizza. It means not just spending time in praise, worship, and prayer with others, but having fun with other people who also love Jesus. Fellowshipping creates an atmosphere to encourage one another, give someone hope, pray for each other, and give glory to God. It is okay to have fun. Just keep it clean. Take time to fellowship.

"Not forsaking the assembling of ourselves together, as the manner of some is; but exhorting one another: and so much the more, as ye see the day approaching," Hebrews 10:25 KJV.

GOOD WORKS means making good choices and doing good toward others. Doing good works does not get you into heaven, but good works will lead others to a relationship with Jesus that will get them into heaven. Good works might be as simple as offering a smile or not taking part in office gossip. It might include giving to a charity or helping your neighbor when the storm knocks down a tree in his yard. Good works might take you on a missionary trip or teaching a class. A good work might be treating someone with respect. There are so many opportunities to do good works that the possibilities are endless. The old 'do to others as you would have them do to you' that momma used to tell you. Well, that fits here. Or the 'what would Jesus do' question. The answer will always be a good work. Show others Christ by choosing to be the bigger person and do a good work even when they don't deserve it.

"Let your light so shine before men, that they may see your good works and glorify your Father in heaven," Matthew 5:16.

Stepping Stones

1. Everyone is born into sin and selfishness.

2. Salvation is deliverance from the power of sin and reuniting with your Creator.

3. Salvation makes you a new creation. You live in the same body and you are aware of the past, but you have an opportunity for a very different future when the Father adopts you and recreates you through salvation.

4. Confess your sin, repent of your sin, be transformed, and live with joy.

5. You are justified, sanctified, and will be glorified in Christ.

6. Jesus is your atonement. He paid the price for all your sin and offers the opportunity to be at one with Father God.

7. Salvation offers redemption (your purchase price from sin), pays propitiation (the cost of God's anger against sin), and renews reconciliation (reuniting you with God so you can live in harmony with Him and spend time with Him).

8. You now have the authority and power to live free from sin.

9. Your life is eternal.

10. Tools to walking in your salvation are reading the Word, praying, spending time with other believers, and making good choices.

There Must Be a Better Way

WALKING IN SALVATION

1. What is salvation?

2. Why do I need salvation?

3. What are the three (3) principal works Christ did for me? Give a brief explanation of each.

4. Complete the Chart using the following choices:

Instant, future, progressive, mortal body to eternal body, human to divine, building character

Spirit	Soul	Body
Justification	Sanctification	Glorification

Glossary

Adultery - The act of being sexually unfaithful to one's spouse

Agape - Affection, goodwill, love, brotherly love, a love feast

Angel - Messenger of God

Apostasy - Turning away from the religion, faith, or principles that one used to believe

Apostle - One sent forth, one chosen and sent with a special commission as a fully authorized representative of the sender.

Atonement - To cover, blot out, forgive; restore harmony between two individuals.

Attribute – An inherent characteristic

Backslide - To go back to ungodly ways of believing or acting.

Blasphemy - Words or actions showing a lack of respect for God or anything sacred.

Bless - To make or call holy, to ask God's favor, to praise; to make happy.

Blessing - A prayer asking God's favor for something, something that brings joy or comfort.

Born-again – To be begotten or birthed from God, the beginning, to start anew

Carnal - Of the flesh or body, not of the spirit, worldly; seat of one's desires opposed to the spirit of Christ

Cherubim - Guardian angels, angels that guard or protect places

Commitment - A promise, a pledge

Conditional - Placing restrictions, conditions, or provisions to receive

Conversion - Turn, return, turn back; change

Convert - To change from one form or use to another, to change from one belief or religion to another.

Courtship - The act or process of seeking the affection of one with the intent of seeking to win a pledge of marriage

Covenant - A pledge, alliance, agreement

Cult - A body of believers whose doctrine denies the deity of Christ.

Deliverance - A freeing or being freed, rescue; the act of change or transformation.

Demon - Evil spirit

Devil - Principal title for satan, the archenemy of God and man

Dispensation - A period of time, sometimes called ages

Dominion - To rule over, have power over, overcome, exercise lordship over

Eros - Erotic, physical love

Eternal - Existing always, forever, without time

Evangelist - Proclaims the gospel of Jesus Christ

Faith - Believing, trusting, depending, and relying on God

Fellowship - Sharing, communion, partnership, intimacy

Forgiveness - To pardon, release from bondage

Fornication - To act like a harlot, to be unfaithful to God, illicit sexual intercourse

Glorification - Salvation of the body, transforming mortal bodies to eternal bodies

Grace - Unmerited favor of God, help given in the time of need from a loving God

Holy - Set apart, sacred

Intercession - To meet or encounter, to strike upon, to pray for another

Justification - Salvation of the spirit, just as if I never sinned

Marriage - A divine institution designed by God as an intimate union, which is physical, emotional, intellectual, social, and most importantly, spiritual

New Testament - Text of the new covenant

Offering - Everything you give beyond your tithe

Old Testament - Text of the old covenant

Omnipotent - All-encompassing power of God

Omnipresent - Unlimited nature of God, ability to be everywhere at all times

Omniscient - God's power to know all things

Pastor - Shepherds of the body of believers

Philia - Conditional love, based on feelings, friendships

Praise - Thanksgiving, to say good things about, words that show approval.

Prayer - Communication with God

Prophet - One who is a spokesperson for God, one who has seen the message of God and declares that message

Propitiation - To satisfy the anger of God, to gain favor; appease

Rapture - To be carried away, or the catching away of

Reconciliation - Restore harmony or fellowship between individuals, to make friendly again

Redemption - To buy back, to purchase, recover, to Rescue from sin

Regeneration - To give new life or force to, renew, to be restored, to make better, improve or reform, to grow back anew

Repent - To give new life or force, to renew, to be restored, to make better, improve or reform, to grow back a new.

Resurrection - A return to life subsequent to death

Revelation - The act of revealing or making known

Righteousness - Right standing with God, integrity, virtue, purity of life, correctness of thinking

Sacrifice - The act of offering something, giving one thing for the sake of another; a loss of profit

Salvation - Deliverance from any kind of evil whether material or spiritual, being saved from danger or evil; to rescue.

Sanctification - Salvation of the soul. Separation from the seduction of sin

Satan - The chief of fallen spirits, opponent; adversary

Sealing - Something that guarantees, a sign or token, to make with a seal to make it official or genuine

Sin - All unrighteousness, missing the mark, wrong or fault; violation of the law

Spirit - A being that is not of this world, has no flesh or bones

Steward - A guardian or overseer of someone else's property, manager

Supernatural - Departing from what is usual, normal, or natural to give the appearance of transcending the laws of nature

Talent - A natural skill that is unusual.

Tithe - Ten percent of all your increase

Tribulation - Distress, trouble, a pressing together, pressure, affliction

Trinity - Three in one: Father, Son, Holy Spirit

Unconditional - No restrictions, conditions, boundaries, demands, or specific provisions

Will – Choice, inclination, desire, pleasure, command, what one wishes or determines shall be done

About the Author

Pamela is a teacher, mentor, and author of the inspirational book *Destiny Arise* and children's books including *Time in a Tuna*. Pam earned her bachelor's degree at the University of Illinois Springfield, her master's degree in Organizational Leadership at Lincoln Christian University, and her doctorate in Leadership at Christian Leadership University. She serves as a mentor for the Spirit Life Circles sponsored by CLU.

She works from her home in the prairie land of central Illinois. Pam and her bodybuilding husband own a gym/fitness center that promotes living a balanced life. She taught sixth grade for almost twenty years. Pam also taught preschool through adult-age students in various venues. She served as director of Super Church, the children's ministry in the United Methodist Church in her hometown. Pam also served in the church nursery, as director of New Life Ministries Discipleship Program, Vacation Bible School Director, Kingdom Kids Children's Ministry Director, and Sunday School teacher. She has also been on missionary trips. Her favorite trip, so far, was the time she spent in Belize.

Pam enjoys kayaking, bicycling, and riding her motor scooter. When she isn't writing, she enjoys spending time with her four children and their families which includes five grandchildren who are the inspiration of her children's books.

Walking with Jesus Series

BECOMING THE BEST ME I CAN BE

Book 1 - There Must Be a Better Way
Walking in Salvation
Book 2 - Lord, I Need Help!
Walking with the Holy Spirit
Book 3 - I Thought I Was Changed
Walking in Transformation
Book 4 - I Am Supernatural
Walking in Spiritual Gifts
Book 5 - I Am Strong
Walking as a Warrior
Book 6 - I Am Fruitful
Walking in the Fruit of the Spirit
Book 7 - Love Letters from God
Walking in the Word
Book 8 - Time in the Garden
Walking in the Power of Prayer
Book 9 - I'm in Charge of What?
Walking in Stewardship
Book 10 - The End of – Well, Pretty Much Everything
Walking into Eternity

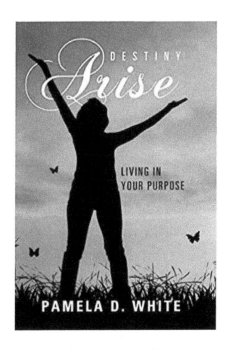

Who am I? What am I doing here? Where am I going? Everyone at some point in life asks these questions. You were wired to ask and engineered to pursue the answers. The road to discovering destiny is besieged by fiascoes, failures, and the agony of defeat. If your strength has been depleted and has caused you to give up, sit down, push pause, and snooze until another day, then this book is just for you! Amazing experiences are waiting for you. Get ready to be awakened from the posture of defeat, depression, and despair.

Destiny Arise is an easy-to-read book, providing tools to aid in living an amazing life. This book is designed as a trip adviser for your expedition. It will teach you how to evict the spirit of mediocrity and use your past to propel you into your future. You will learn how to shake off the common, arising to be an uncommon force taking your rightful place in the earth. You can change the world. I pray this book will ignite a passionate fire to pursue your destiny unapologetically. Destiny, awake from your slumber and arise.

CPSIA information can be obtained
at www.ICGtesting.com
Printed in the USA
LVHW021947020122
707668LV00015B/436

9 781737 080206